Keyboards

Wendy Lynch

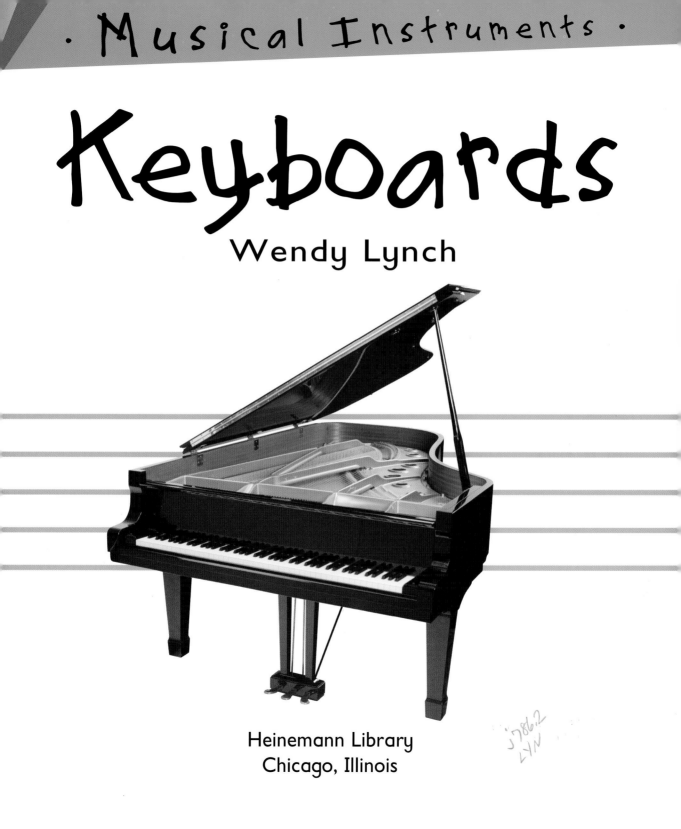

Heinemann Library
Chicago, Illinois

© 2002 Reed Educational & Professional Publishing
Published by Heinemann Library,
an imprint of Reed Educational & Professional Publishing,
Chicago, Illinois

Customer Service 888-454-2279

Visit our website at www.heinemannlibrary.com

Designed by Visual Image
Illustrations by Jane Watkins
Originated by Dot Gradations
Printed and bound in South China

06 05 04 03 02
10 9 8 7 6 5 4 3 2 1

Library of Congress Cataloging-in-Publication Data
Lynch, Wendy, 1945-
    Keyboards / Wendy Lynch.
       p. cm. -- (Musical instruments)
    Includes bibliographical references (p.   ) and index.
    ISBN 1-58810-234-3
    1. Keyboard instruments--Juvenile literature. [1. Keyboard
instruments. 2. Piano.] I. Title. II. Series.
    ML549 .L96 2001
    786'.19--dc21

                         2001000096

Acknowledgments
The publishers would like to thank the following for permission to reproduce photographs: p. 4 Zefa/ Powerstock; pp. 5, 27 Patrick Ford/Redferns; pp. 6, 7, 18, 19 Photodisc; pp. 9, 28, 29 Gareth Boden; pp. 10, 21 Robert Harding; p. 11 Ace Photo Agency; p. 14 Redferns; p. 15 Trevor Clifford; p. 16 Ian Shaw/ Stone; p. 17 David Farrell/Lebrecht collection; pp. 20, 23 Corbis; p. 22 Stone; p. 24 Superstock; p. 25 Ebet Roberts/Redferns; p. 26 Kate Mount/Lebrecht collection.
Cover photograph reproduced with permission of Photodisc.
Special thanks to Susan Lerner for her comments in the preparation of this book.
Every effort has been made to contact copyright holders of any material reproduced in this book. Any omissions will be rectified in subsequent printings if notice is given to the publisher.

Some words are shown in bold, **like this.** You can find out what they mean by looking in the glossary.

Contents

Making Music Together

There are many musical instruments in the world. Each instrument makes a different sound. We can make music together by playing these instruments in a band or an **orchestra.**

Bands and orchestras are made up
of different groups of instruments.
One of these groups is called keyboard
instruments. They are often found in
smaller bands like this **jazz** band.

5

What Are Keyboard Instruments?

The piano, the organ, the harpsichord, and the **synthesizer** are all keyboard instruments. They are called keyboard instruments because they are played using a keyboard.

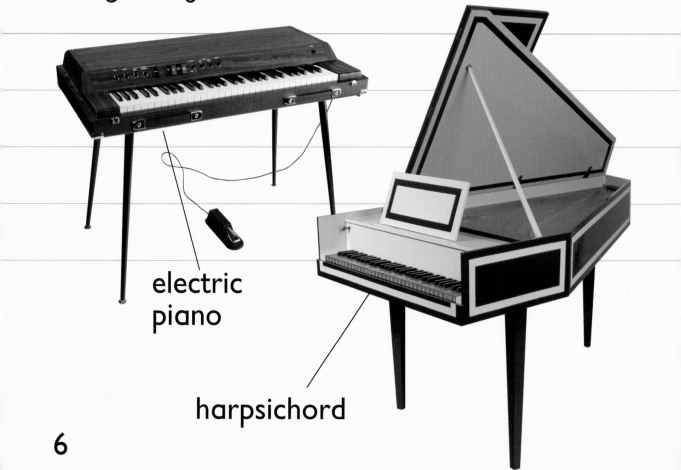

electric piano

harpsichord

A keyboard has many small parts called keys. You press or hit a key to make a sound. Each key makes a different sound, or musical note.

organ   grand piano

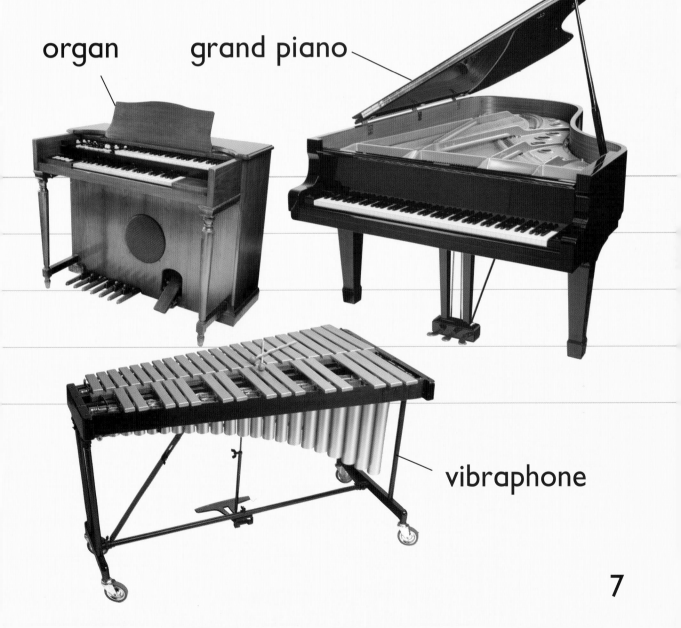

vibraphone

The Piano

The piano is a popular keyboard instrument. Children often learn to play it in school or with a private teacher.

You can play the piano alone or with another person. Music for two players is called a piano duet. One player plays the keys on the left of the keyboard. The other plays the keys on the right.

Making a Sound

The piano has black keys and white keys, arranged in a pattern. The keys on the left of the keyboard play notes with lower **pitch.** The keys on the right play higher notes.

Inside the piano, there are **strings** for each key. When you press a key, a hammer hits the string. The strings that play the lower notes are thicker than the strings for the higher notes.

How the Sound Is Made

When a hammer hits a **string** inside the piano, the string begins to move quickly from side to side. This movement is called **vibration.**

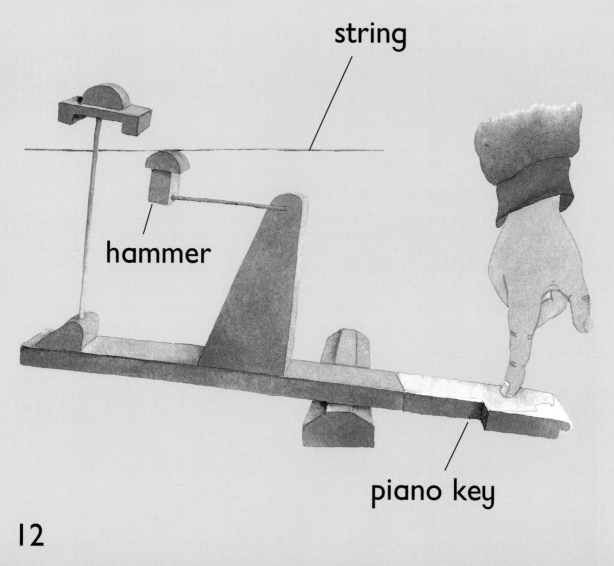

string

hammer

piano key

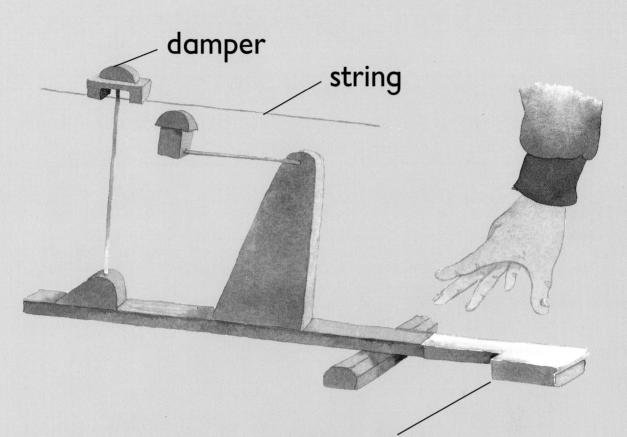

damper

string

piano key

The movement of the strings makes the air inside the piano vibrate. This makes the sound. When you lift your finger, a piece of padded wood called a damper stops the string's vibration.

13

Types of Pianos

The **upright piano** is a popular piano. It takes up less space than some other pianos. You can find upright pianos in schools, in houses, and in public places like cafés and restaurants.

Grand pianos are often played in concerts. If you keep the lid open as you play, the sound will be stronger and richer. More air can **vibrate,** and the sound can travel farther.

Piano Concerts

In school, your teacher may play the piano to **accompany** singing, dancing, or movement activities. Your teacher may also play the piano for a **musical** or concert you perform.

You may hear the piano on its own or with other musical instruments. This piano **trio** includes a piano, a violin, and a cello.

Types of Keyboards

The harpsichord has **strings** inside it, like the piano. When you press a key, a small piece of wood inside the harpsichord **plucks** a string.

The electric piano sounds a lot like an **upright piano,** but it does not make music using strings and hammers. An electronic **amplifier** makes the sound.

Organs and Harmoniums

The organ has a keyboard, but it also uses air. Each key is connected to a pipe. When you press a key, air is forced into a pipe and **vibrates** to make a sound. Bigger pipes have lower **pitch.**

The harmonium is a kind of organ with **bellows** that hold air. As you touch the keys, you also press a foot pedal. This pedal pumps air into a **reed,** causing vibration and making a sound.

The Wider Family

To play the accordion, you press both keys and buttons. At the same time, you push and pull the **bellows** to make air move inside the accordion. The **vibrating** air makes the sound.

The vibraphone has metal bars that look like a keyboard. You strike the bars using two hammers called mallets. You can hear the vibraphone in **jazz.**

Famous Musicians and Composers

The famous **composer** Wolfgang Amadeus Mozart started to study piano when he was four years old. Mozart wrote a lot of music for the piano.

Stevie Wonder is a famous keyboard player. Although he is blind, he learned to play the piano when he was very young. He also sings and writes songs.

Keyboard Music Today

People play electronic keyboards in **jazz, rock,** and **pop** music today. Many keyboards can play tunes and drum **rhythms.** Keyboards can be linked to computers to play many new sounds.

You can also hear the **synthesizer** in rock and pop music. Synthesizers can **imitate** the sounds of many different instruments. Jean-Michel Jarre uses synthesizers and lasers in his concerts.

Sound Activities

You can make up your own music on the piano. Make up some music that sounds like rain falling. Make it slow and gentle, then faster and louder. Can you make a sound like thunder?

Ask a grown-up to lift the lid of a piano. Then ask the person to play some notes. Stand on a chair and look inside the piano. Can you see the hammers hit the **strings?**

Thinking about Keyboards

You can find the answers to all of these questions in this book.

1. Why are the instruments in this book called keyboard instruments?

2. What is a piano duet?

3. How does a piano make and stop its sound?

4. What is the difference between how the sounds of a piano and an organ are made?

5. How do you play the accordion?

6. What is a vibraphone?

Glossary

accompany to play along with someone else

amplifier something that changes electrical signals into sounds by sending them through a speaker

bellows pump used to push air into the soundpipes of an instrument

composer person who writes music

imitate to copy

jazz style of music that is often made up as it is played

musical play set to music, with songs and dancing

orchestra large group of musicians who play their instruments together

pitch highness or lowness of a sound or musical note

pluck to pull

pop popular music

reed thin strip of cane or metal

rhythm pattern of repeated beats or sounds

rock kind of pop music with a strong beat

string part of a piano, made of steel wire, that is hit to make a sound

synthesizer electronic instrument that can make or change many different sounds

trio group of three musicians, or a piece of music written for three players

upright piano piano in which the strings stand up against the soundboard

vibrate to move up and down or from side to side very quickly

More Books to Read

Harris, Pamela K. *Pianos*. Chanhassen, Minn.: The Child's World, Incorporated, 2000.

Kalman, Bobbie. *Musical Instruments from A to Z*. New York: Crabtree Publishing Company, 1997.

Turner, Barrie Carson. *Modern Instruments*. North Mankato, Minn.: Smart Apple Media, 2000.

Index